This book is a collaboration between
Fondation Ipsen and Mayo Clinic.

The story has been inspired by
Gifty's experience with depression.

The words in bold refer to key terms on page 32.

MEDICAL EDITOR
Paul E. Croarkin, D.O., M.S., Consultant, Psychiatry and Psychology, Children's Center,
Mayo Clinic, Rochester, MN; Professor of Psychiatry, Mayo Clinic College of Medicine and Science;
in collaboration with Kelly A. Rentfrow, L.G.S.W., M.S.W., Social Worker, Department of Pediatric
and Adolescent Medicine, Mayo Clinic, Rochester, MN

SERIES CONCEPTION
Fredric B. Meyer, M.D., Consultant, Department of Neurologic Surgery, Mayo Clinic,
Rochester, MN; Executive Dean of Education, Professor of Neurosurgery,
Mayo Clinic College of Medicine and Science

James A. Levine, M.D., Ph.D., Professor, President, Fondation Ipsen, Paris, France

My Life Beyond

DEPRESSION

A Mayo Clinic patient story
by Hey Gee and Gifty

Foreword

Gifty, who helped create this story, has had **depression** since she was young. For her, it may be caused in part by living in a community with very little diversity and being physically disabled from a stroke early in her life. She is not able to participate in many of the activities that her peers do. She'd like to play sports such as soccer, volleyball and basketball, and to dance and act in plays. Her disability makes this very difficult and she feels left out of almost everything. She is 15 years old and wants to hang out with her friends, but her friends do not live in her small town. Her family is looking for a school that might better fit her needs, and moving to an area with more diversity and better resources is a possibility.

Gifty does have a good support system in her family and older friends who have similar interests, including social activism, poetry and music. She has also been able to reconnect with her birth family in Liberia, and she hopes to return in the next few years.

Gifty's life has been challenging for sure, but she is and always has been a fighter. She is an inspiration to all who know and love her.

Gifty's mom

"

THERE IS NO WAVE THAT IS TOO BIG TO HANDLE

"

HELLO, I'M BINDU. I AM 12 AND I'VE HAD **DEPRESSION** SINCE I WAS LITTLE. **DEPRESSION** IS A **MOOD DISORDER** THAT AFFECTS HOW YOU THINK AND FEEL.

EVERYONE FEELS SAD SOMETIMES. BUT WITH **DEPRESSION**, THOSE FEELINGS MAY SEEM TOO BIG TO HANDLE A LOT OF THE TIME.

DEPRESSION AFFECTS EVERYONE DIFFERENTLY. YOU MIGHT FEEL SAD OR OVERWHELMED A LOT OF THE TIME. YOU MAY NOT ENJOY THE USUAL THINGS AS MUCH ANYMORE, LIKE SPENDING TIME WITH FRIENDS, PARTICIPATING IN SCHOOL, OR PLAYING SPORTS OR DOING OTHER ACTIVITIES.

DEPRESSION MAY BE CAUSED BY DIFFERENT THINGS. YOU MIGHT HAVE INHERITED TRAITS THAT MAKE **DEPRESSION** MORE LIKELY. DIFFERENCES INSIDE YOUR BODY OR WHAT'S HAPPENING AROUND YOU MAY CAUSE **DEPRESSION** TOO.

IF YOU HAVE **DEPRESSION** AS A KID OR A TEENAGER, YOU MAY FEEL IRRITABLE OR ANGRY AND ACT OUT. YOU MAY FEEL OR THINK BAD THINGS ABOUT YOURSELF OR EVEN WANT TO HURT YOURSELF. IT MIGHT ALSO AFFECT HOW MUCH YOU EAT OR HOW WELL YOU SLEEP.

FOR SOME PEOPLE WITH **DEPRESSION**, THE FEELINGS AND THOUGHTS ARE SO BAD THAT THEY WANT TO DIE. I HAVEN'T FELT THIS WAY, BUT I KNOW IF I EVER DO, IT'S VERY IMPORTANT TO TELL MY PARENTS AND THERAPISTS ABOUT IT RIGHT AWAY AND START GETTING MORE HELP. ANYONE CAN USE THE 988 SUICIDE & CRISIS LIFELINE BY CALLING OR TEXTING 988.

TREATMENT MAY INVOLVE TAKING MEDICATION AND TALKING WITH A THERAPIST. MEDICATION CAN HELP RESTORE HEALTHY BRAIN FUNCTION, SO YOU THINK AND FEEL BETTER.

I MEET WITH A THERAPIST ON A REGULAR BASIS. **THERAPY** HAS HELPED ME UNDERSTAND HOW **DEPRESSION** IMPACTS MY LIFE, AND I'VE LEARNED WAYS TO **COPE** THAT HELP ME HAVE HEALTHIER THOUGHTS AND FEELINGS.

AND I START TO FEEL BETTER.

AND SOMETIMES, WHEN I'M ALONE, I HAVE DARK THOUGHTS ... I REALLY CAN'T CONTROL IT.

IT'S LIKE DARK CLOUDS ARE BLOCKING THE LIGHT FROM THE SUN.

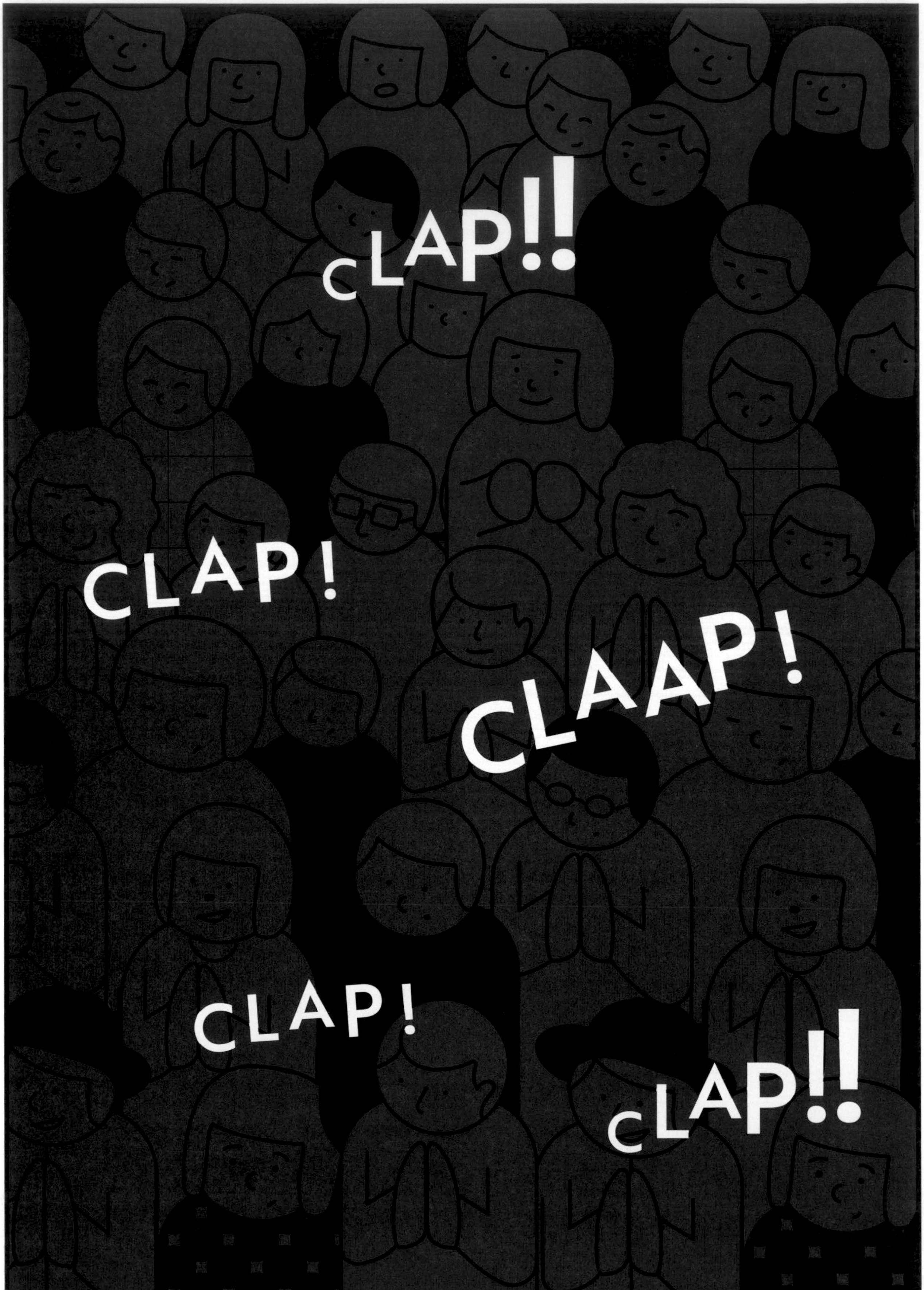
CLAP!!
CLAP!
CLAAP!
CLAP!
CLAP!!

KEY TERMS

antidepressant: a medication that is used to help the brain and body with depression. Commonly used groups (classes) of antidepressants include selective serotonin reuptake inhibitors (SSRIs), serotonin-norepinephrine reuptake inhibitors (SNRIs), tricyclic antidepressants and monoamine oxidase inhibitors (MAOIs).

cope: to deal with or manage thoughts, feelings or situations that are stressful

depression: a mood disorder that typically causes sadness that lasts a long time or happens frequently and involves loss of interest in usual activities

meditation: clearing and calming the mind by focusing attention on your breathing, a word or phrase, or a visualization

mental illness: a medical problem that affects your mood, thinking and behavior, with symptoms that are long-lasting or frequent and get in the way of your life. Examples of mental illness include depression, anxiety disorders, schizophrenia, eating disorders and addictive behaviors.

mood disorder: a mental illness in which your mood and feelings don't match up with your circumstances, and this gets in the way of your ability to function and cope

suicidal thoughts and suicide: severely depressed thoughts and behaviors that can result in ending your own life

symptoms: feelings (such as pain or anxiety) or changes in your body (such as weight gain) that result from a disease, injury or health condition

therapy: talking about your situation with a mental health provider to help you cope and to reduce the symptoms of a mental illness. This type of talk therapy is also called psychotherapy.

MORE INFORMATION FROM THE MEDICAL EDITOR

By **Paul E. Croarkin, D.O., M.S.**
Consultant, Psychiatry and Psychology, Children's Center, Mayo Clinic, Rochester, MN; Professor of Psychiatry, Mayo Clinic College of Medicine and Science; in collaboration with Kelly A. Rentfrow, L.G.S.W., M.S.W., Social Worker, Department of Pediatric and Adolescent Medicine, Mayo Clinic, Rochester, MN

Depression is a **mood disorder** that affects how you think and feel. It often involves a long period of sadness, and you might lose interest in activities you usually enjoy, such as spending time with friends, playing sports, practicing music or doing other hobbies. This **mood disorder** affects a growing number of children and teens. In the United States in 2020, about 2.4 million people ages 3 to 17 had been diagnosed with **depression**.

Many things may cause or contribute to **depression**. There may be events happening in your life, called environmental or psychosocial factors. Genes you inherited and differences in your body are important too. Those are called genetic or biological factors.

Depression may show up differently in kids or teens, compared with adults. It may lead to behavioral outbursts, irritability, negative feelings or thoughts about themselves, and self-harm, such as cutting. Everyone's mood has highs and lows. But it becomes a concern when it starts to interfere with overall functioning. For example, missing school frequently or not wanting to spend any time with other people may be signs of **depression**. Appetite and sleep patterns can also be impacted.

For some people, their negative thoughts and feelings become so bad that they want to die. They may try to hurt themselves or attempt **suicide**. But this isn't true for everyone with **depression**.

Help is available. **Depression** is a **mental illness**, and it can get better with treatment. Research shows that combining **therapy** and medication typically gives the best results.

To get the most help from **therapy**, find a therapist you feel comfortable and safe with. **Therapy** might include psychotherapy, which involves meeting with a licensed mental health provider for structured sessions to learn strategies to address **depression symptoms**. Therapists will often use cognitive behavioral therapy (CBT) strategies too. CBT helps people identify their negative thought patterns and learn effective coping strategies to address them.

There are many medication options to treat **depression**. The most frequently used medications are called selective serotonin reuptake inhibitors (SSRIs). Some common examples of these include escitalopram (Lexapro), sertraline (Zoloft) and fluoxetine (Prozac). Other classes of medication that are used to treat **depression** include serotonin-norepinephrine reuptake inhibitors (SNRIs), tricyclic **antidepressants**, and monoamine oxidase inhibitors (MAOIs). Typically, your doctor will work with you to find the medication that is best for you. Many people need to try several medications before finding a good fit.

How does medication help with **depression**? Researchers haven't figured this out precisely. They do know that the brain helps to regulate emotions and behaviors. When you are depressed, your brain is not functioning properly, and regulation becomes difficult. Some experts believe that an imbalance of certain chemicals in the brain can lead to **depression symptoms**. The goal of medication would be to target these imbalances. You may need to be patient. The benefits of taking **antidepressant** medications happen slowly, over several weeks. And it's important to not stop taking your **antidepressant** medication without talking with your doctor, even after you feel better.

If you have thoughts about hurting yourself, hurting someone else, dying or **suicide**, especially if the thoughts are new or worse, it's important ask for help right away. In the United States, the 988 Suicide and Crisis Lifeline provides free, confidential support to help you or someone else. You can call or text 988 or visit *988lifeline.org* anytime.

REFERENCES

Lebrun-Harris LA, et al. Five-Year Trends in US Children's Health and Well-being, 2016-2020. *JAMA Pediatrics*. 2022. doi:10.1001/jamapediatrics.2022.0056.

Walter HJ, et al. Clinical practice guideline for the assessment and treatment of children and adolescents with major and persistent depressive disorders. *Journal of the American Academy of Child and Adolescent Psychiatry*. 2022; doi:10.1016/j.jaac.2022.10.001.

WEB RESOURCES

988 Suicide & Crisis Lifeline — https://988lifeline.org
The 988 Suicide & Crisis Lifeline is a national network of local crisis centers that provides free and confidential emotional support to people in suicidal crisis or emotional distress 24 hours a day, 7 days a week in the United States. It aims to advance suicide prevention by empowering people, supporting those who want to help others and building awareness.

Depression & Mood Disorders, Child Mind Institute — https://childmind.org/topics/ depression-mood-disorders
The Child Mind Institute's website includes clear information on different types of depression and other mood disorders, tips for supporting someone with depression, guidance on finding helpful treatment, real-life stories, and more.

ABOUT THE MEDICAL EDITOR

Paul E. Croarkin, D.O., M.S.
Consultant, Psychiatry and Psychology, Children's Center, Mayo Clinic, Rochester, MN;
Professor of Psychiatry, Mayo Clinic College of Medicine and Science; in collaboration with
Kelly A. Rentfrow, L.G.S.W., M.S.W., Social Worker, Department of Pediatric and Adolescent
Medicine, Mayo Clinic, Rochester, MN

Dr. Croarkin is a professor of psychiatry whose work is focused on understanding the neurobiology, optimal treatment and classification of **mood disorders** in children and adolescents. This includes studies of repetitive transcranial magnetic stimulation (rTMS) for adolescent major depressive disorder; collaborative clinical trials; studies of neurophysiology with magnetic resonance spectroscopy (MRS); and novel, single- and paired-pulse transcranial magnetic stimulation (TMS) paradigms. A central theme among Dr. Croarkin's research is investigating the role of certain neurotransmitter systems in early-onset **mood disorders** so that safer and more effective treatments can be developed.

ABOUT THE AUTHORS

Guillaume Federighi, aka **Hey Gee**, is a French and American author and illustrator. He began his career in 1998 in Paris, France. He also spent a few decades exploring the world of street art and graffiti in different European capitals. After moving to New York in 2008, he worked with many companies and brands, developing a reputation in graphic design and illustration for his distinctive style of translating complex ideas into simple and timeless visual stories.
He is also the owner and creative director of Hey Gee Studio, a full-service creative agency based in New York City.

Gifty was born in 2007 in the Tobandu Refugee Camp in Sierra Leone. At birth she had problems with her liver. It soon became clear she would need a liver transplant to survive. This was not a possibility where she lived. Her only chance for survival was to be adopted to a country where she could have the surgery. With the help of an international organization, she was able to find a family in the United States and receive a transplant at age 2 1/2. However, five days after the transplant, Gifty had a massive hemorrhagic stroke. She was brought back in for emergency brain surgery. The stroke left her with physical disabilities and some cognitive impairment. Now a teenager, Gifty likes listening to music, writing poetry, creating fashion designs and taking part in social activism. Her hope and dreams are to have a place in this world and to find peace within herself.

ABOUT FONDATION IPSEN BOOKLAB

Fondation Ipsen improves the lives of millions of people around the world by rethinking scientific communication. The truthful transmission of science to the public is complex because scientific information is often technical and there is a lot of inaccurate information. In 2018, Fondation Ipsen established BookLab to address this need. BookLab books come about through collaboration between scientists, doctors, artists, authors, and children. In paper and electronic formats, and in several languages, BookLab delivers books across more than 50 countries for people of all ages and cultures. Fondation Ipsen BookLab's publications are free of charge to schools, libraries and people living in precarious situations. Join us! Access and share our books by visiting: www.fondation-ipsen.org.

ABOUT MAYO CLINIC PRESS

Launched in 2019, Mayo Clinic Press shines a light on the most fascinating stories in medicine and empowers individuals with the knowledge to build healthier, happier lives. From the award-winning *Mayo Clinic Health Letter* to books and media covering the scope of human health and wellness, Mayo Clinic Press publications provide readers with reliable and trusted content by some of the world's leading health care professionals. Proceeds benefit important medical research and education at Mayo Clinic. For more information about Mayo Clinic Press, visit MCPress.MayoClinic.org.

ABOUT THE COLLABORATION

The My Life Beyond series was developed in partnership between Fondation Ipsen's BookLab and Mayo Clinic, which has provided world-class medical education for more than 150 years. This collaboration aims to provide trustworthy, impactful resources for understanding childhood diseases and other problems that can affect children's well-being.

The series offers readers a holistic perspective of children's lives with — and beyond — their medical challenges. In creating these books, young people who have been Mayo Clinic patients worked together with author-illustrator Hey Gee, sharing their personal experiences. The resulting fictionalized stories authentically bring to life the patients' emotions and their inspiring responses to challenging circumstances. In addition, Mayo Clinic physicians contributed the latest medical expertise on each topic so that these stories can best help other patients, families and caregivers understand how children perceive and work through their own challenges.

Text: Hey Gee and Gifty
Illustrations: Hey Gee

Medical editor: Paul E. Croarkin, D.O., M.S., Consultant, Psychiatry and Psychology, Children's Center, Mayo Clinic, Rochester, MN; Professor of Psychiatry, Mayo Clinic College of Medicine and Science; in collaboration with Kelly A. Rentfrow, L.G.S.W., M.S.W., Social Worker, Department of Pediatric and Adolescent Medicine, Mayo Clinic, Rochester, MN

Managing editor: Anna Cavallo, Health Education and Content Services/Mayo Clinic Press, Mayo Clinic, Rochester, MN
Project manager: Kim Chandler, Department of Education, Mayo Clinic, Rochester, MN
Manager of publications: Céline Colombier-Maffre, Fondation Ipsen, Paris, France
President: James A. Levine, M.D., Ph.D., Professor, Fondation Ipsen, Paris, France

MAYO CLINIC PRESS
200 First St. SW
Rochester, MN 55905
mcpress.mayoclinic.org

For bulk sales to employers, member groups and health-related companies, contact Mayo Clinic, 200 First St. SW, Rochester, MN 55905, or send an email to SpecialSalesMayoBooks@mayo.edu.

Proceeds from the sale of every book benefit important medical research and education at Mayo Clinic.

ISBN 978-1-945564-68-0

Library of Congress Control Number: 2022942495

Printed in the United States of America